STREAM

NAVIGATING YOUR CAREER JOURNEY

SARVJEET KUMAR

Made with ♥ on the Notion Press Platform
www.notionpress.com

"Dedicated to my incredible students and parents,

You are the inspiration behind these pages, the driving force that fuels my passion for teaching and writing. Your curiosity, dedication, and unwavering belief in the pursuit of knowledge have enriched my life in ways I could have never imagined. This book is a testament to your boundless potential, and I dedicate it to each and every one of you. May it serve as a reminder that education knows no bounds and that your dreams are within reach.

Special Thanks to Arindam Dasgupta, Aarav,Aman Raj, Subham, Abhisek, Suman

With gratitude and admiration,

Sarvjeet Kumar

Contents

Foreword

In a world brimming with possibilities, choosing the right career path after Class 10 can be a daunting task. "Stream" offers invaluable guidance for students and parents alike, helping them make informed decisions about selecting the right stream for their future. Packed with insights, real-life stories, and expert advice, this book is a roadmap to discovering one's passions, strengths, and the perfect career trajectory. Embark on a transformative journey towards a fulfilling and prosperous future with "Stream."

Preface

The journey from Class 10 to the precipice of higher education is an exhilarating and sometimes overwhelming experience. It is a phase where we stand on the brink of shaping our future, where the choices we make can influence the course of our lives. As educators and mentors, we have witnessed the uncertainties, anxieties, and aspirations that students and parents grapple with during this critical juncture.

"Stream: Navigating Your Career Journey " was born from the recognition that making informed decisions about one's academic path is a cornerstone of a successful and fulfilling future. This book aims to provide a comprehensive guide that not only addresses the pragmatic aspects of stream selection but also delves into the profound question of personal identity and passion.

In these pages, you will find a tapestry of perspectives and experiences. We have drawn from the wisdom of educators, career counselors, and professionals who have generously shared their insights. Real-life stories of individuals who have successfully navigated the maze of career choices serve as beacons of inspiration. We have strived to offer practical advice that empowers you to explore your interests, discover your strengths, and make choices that align with your goals.

Our heartfelt gratitude goes to the countless students, parents, and educators whose experiences and questions have shaped the content of this book. We dedicate "Stream" to you, with the hope that it will illuminate the path ahead and instill in you the belief that your dreams are attainable.

May this book serve as a source of guidance, inspiration, and empowerment as you step into the exciting world of higher education and career exploration. Your journey begins here, and we are honored to be a part of it.

Warm regards,
Sarvjeet Kumar
2024

Acknowledgements

The creation of "Stream: Navigating Your Career Journey" has been a labor of love and a collaborative effort that would not have been possible without the support, contributions, and dedication of many individuals and organizations.

First and foremost, we extend our heartfelt gratitude to the students and parents whose questions, stories, and aspirations have been the driving force behind this book. Your curiosity, enthusiasm, and willingness to share your experiences have been an endless source of inspiration.

We are immensely thankful to the educators, career counselors, and professionals who generously shared their knowledge, expertise, and insights. Your wisdom has enriched the content of this book and made it a valuable resource for students and parents alike.

We extend our thanks to our publishers, editors, and the entire team involved in bringing this book to life. Your dedication to quality and commitment to our vision have been instrumental in making "Stream" a reality.

Lastly, we are deeply indebted to all those who believe in the power of education and the potential of every student to achieve their dreams. Your commitment to nurturing young minds and guiding them towards a brighter future is a testament to the importance of education in shaping our world.

To all those mentioned and countless others who have played a role, however small or significant, in the creation of "Stream," we offer our heartfelt appreciation. This book stands as a collective effort to empower the next generation, and your contributions have made it possible.

Prologue

As we conclude this book, "Stream: Navigating Your Career Journey," we reflect on the journey we have embarked upon together. This book was conceived with the intention of providing guidance and clarity to students and parents facing the pivotal decision of selecting a career path. It aimed to demystify the complexities surrounding stream selection and empower individuals to make informed choices aligned with their aspirations.

Throughout these pages, we have explored a myriad of topics, from understanding the different streams available to uncovering one's passions, strengths, and interests. We have delved into the importance of self-discovery, the role of mentors, and the significance of resilience in the face of challenges.

It is our sincere hope that "Stream" has served as a valuable resource for you, offering not just practical advice but also the encouragement to dream big and pursue your ambitions. We trust that the stories shared within these pages have inspired you to believe in the power of education and the potential within yourself.

Remember, the journey of self-discovery and career exploration is ongoing. This book is a starting point, a compass to guide you in the right direction. As you progress through your educational and professional endeavors, continue to seek knowledge, embrace change, and adapt to the evolving landscape of opportunities.

We encourage you to stay curious, remain open to new experiences, and never lose sight of your goals. Surround yourself with mentors and peers who inspire and support you. Most importantly, have faith in your abilities and the unique path you are forging.

In closing, we express our deepest gratitude to all the readers who have taken this journey with us. Your commitment to personal growth and the pursuit of knowledge is a testament to your potential to shape a brighter future. We are honored to have been a part of your educational and career exploration, and we wish you all the success and fulfillment in your chosen path.

As you continue on your career journey, may you find joy in learning, resilience in adversity, and the satisfaction of realizing your dreams.

With warm regards,
Sarvjeet Kumar

CHAPTER ONE

Introduction

"Stream" is not just about choosing a subject; it is about discovering who you are and what you aspire to be. It emphasizes the importance of self-reflection and the value of seeking guidance from mentors, parents, and peers. We hope that as you turn the pages of this book, you will find clarity, purpose, and the confidence to embark on your unique career journey.

In the journey of life, there are few crossroads as significant as the one that arrives at the conclusion of Class 10. It's a juncture where the roads of childhood merge into the thoroughfares of adulthood, where the decisions made can shape the course of one's future. This is the point where the educational system in many countries, including India, presents students with a critical choice: the selection of an academic stream.

In the vast landscape of education, this decision often appears as a daunting puzzle. Science, Commerce, Arts, or Vocational? Which path will lead to the destination of your dreams? The weight of this choice can be felt not only by students but also by their parents and mentors, who strive to provide the best possible guidance.

"Pathways to Success: Navigating Your Career Journey After Class 10" is a compass for those standing at this intersection of choice. It is a guidebook designed to shed light on the multifaceted world of stream selection and provide insights into the opportunities and challenges that lie ahead. Whether you are a student contemplating your options or a parent seeking to support your child's decision, this book offers valuable perspectives and practical advice to navigate this crucial phase.

Within these pages, you will discover stories of individuals who have journeyed through various streams, anecdotes of triumphs and setbacks, and a wealth of knowledge from experienced educators and career counselors. This book is not just about selecting a stream; it is about understanding yourself, your passions, your strengths, and aligning them with your aspirations.

In the chapters that follow, we will explore the intricacies of each academic stream, dissecting the subjects, exploring career prospects, and unraveling the skills required to excel. We will delve into the role of self-assessment, the influence of societal expectations, and the importance of seeking guidance from mentors. "Pathways to Success" aims to empower you with the information and confidence needed to make an informed decision.

While this book provides guidance, it also encourages you to embrace the journey of self-discovery. Your educational path is a personal expedition, and it is okay to explore, adapt, and grow along the way. Our goal is not just to prepare you for a career but to equip you with the skills and mindset to navigate a dynamic and ever-changing world.

As you embark on this odyssey of choices, challenges, and achievements, remember that each step you take contributes to your growth and the realization of your dreams. "Pathways to Success" is your companion on this voyage, helping you chart a course towards a fulfilling and prosperous future.

May your journey be filled with self-discovery, resilience, and the joy of pursuing your passions. Your pathway to success begins here.

CHAPTER TWO

Dreams, Goals, Careers, and Degrees

Dreams, goals, careers, and degrees—these words are often thrown around in conversations about education and future aspirations. But what do they really mean, and how do they relate to one another? In this chapter, we will dive deep into the definitions of these terms and explore the nuanced differences between them, using real-life examples to shed light on their significance.

Dreams: The Seeds of Aspiration

Let's start with dreams. Dreams are the seeds of aspiration, the vivid mental images of what you hope to achieve or experience in your lifetime. They are deeply personal and can encompass a wide range of desires, from personal fulfillment to societal impact. Dreams often ignite our passion, providing a sense of purpose and direction in life.

Dreams are the idealized, imaginative visions of what you want to achieve, become, or experience in the future.

Example: Imagine a young artist who dreams of traveling the world, painting landscapes in remote and exotic locations, and sharing her unique perspective through her art. Her dream encapsulates her desire for creative expression, exploration, and cultural immersion.

Goals: The Building Blocks of Achievement

Goals are the practical steps we take to turn our dreams into reality. They are the specific, measurable, and actionable targets that guide our actions and decisions. Goals serve as the roadmap toward the realization of our dreams, breaking down the grand vision into manageable milestones.

Goals are specific, measurable, and time-bound targets that align with our dreams and aspirations.

Example: Continuing with our artist's dream, her goals might include enrolling in an art school, mastering specific techniques, saving money for travel, and planning exhibitions to showcase her work. Each goal is a stepping stone toward her dream of becoming a renowned artist.

Careers: The Pathways of Purpose

Careers are the paths we choose to follow in our professional lives. They encompass the series of connected employment opportunities, roles, and activities that provide us with a source of income and contribute to our personal growth and development. Careers are shaped by our interests, skills, and goals.

Careers are the long-term pursuits that involve a series of connected jobs and roles, aligning with our passions, talents, and aspirations.

Example: Let's consider a dedicated medical student who aspires to become a surgeon. Her career path involves years of rigorous education, internships, and specialized training. Her ultimate goal is to save lives and make a significant impact on the field of medicine.

Degrees: The Credentials of Expertise

Degrees are the formal qualifications and certifications awarded by educational institutions upon successful completion of a program or course of study. They are a tangible representation of one's knowledge and expertise in a particular field. Degrees open doors to career opportunities and serve as evidence of one's commitment to learning and specialization.

Degrees are formal credentials awarded by educational institutions to individuals who have successfully completed a prescribed course of study, indicating expertise in a specific area.

Example: Consider a computer science enthusiast who earns a bachelor's degree in computer engineering. This degree serves as proof of his proficiency in programming, algorithms, and computer systems, enhancing his career prospects in the tech industry.

Differentiating Dreams, Goals, Careers, and Degrees

Now that we have defined these terms, let's explore their differences with the help of real-life examples:

Dream vs. Goal: Dreams are the broad, overarching visions that give us purpose, while goals are the actionable steps that help us realize those dreams. For instance, if someone dreams of making a meaningful impact on environmental conservation, their goal might be to lead a community-based recycling initiative.

Goal vs. Career: Goals are specific targets that contribute to our long-term career aspirations. A goal might be to attain a management position within five years, aligning with a career path in business administration.

Career vs. Degree: A career is the ongoing journey of professional pursuits, while a degree is the formal qualification that often kickstarts or advances a career. An individual pursuing a career in psychology might earn a master's degree to become a licensed therapist.

Degree vs. Dream: Degrees are formal qualifications, and dreams are aspirational visions. However, they can intersect when someone's dream involves achieving a specific level of education. For instance, a dream of becoming a renowned scientist may include obtaining a Ph.D. to pursue groundbreaking research.

The Interplay of Dreams, Goals, Careers, and Degrees

It's important to note that these concepts are not isolated; they interweave throughout our lives. Dreams inspire our goals, which, in turn, shape our careers and the degrees we pursue. The dynamic relationship between these elements reflects the evolving nature of our ambitions and the diverse pathways to success.

Consider the story of Malala Yousafzai, the Pakistani activist and Nobel laureate. Her dream was to ensure that every girl received an education. Her goals included speaking out for girls' rights and advocating for education. Her career as an activist emerged from her dedication to this cause, and while she didn't earn a formal degree in activism, her actions and impact speak volumes about her expertise in advocating for education.

In conclusion, understanding the distinctions between dreams, goals, careers, and degrees is crucial for anyone embarking on a journey of self-discovery and achievement. By clarifying your dreams, setting meaningful goals, pursuing a fulfilling career, and acquiring relevant degrees, you can navigate the intricate tapestry of your aspirations and create a life rich with purpose and accomplishment. As you progress through this book, you'll gain further insights into how these elements can harmonize to shape your unique path to success.

CHAPTER THREE

Discovering Your Path: The Power of Self-Exploration

In the previous chapter, we explored the fundamental concepts of dreams, goals, careers, and degrees. We learned that dreams are the seeds of aspiration, goals are the building blocks of achievement, careers are the pathways of purpose, and degrees are the credentials of expertise. But how do you ensure that your dreams align with your goals, your career path resonates with your passions, and your pursuit of degrees is guided by a deeper understanding of yourself? The answer lies in the powerful process of self-discovery.

The Crucial Role of Self-Discovery

Imagine setting off on a road trip to an unknown destination without a map or GPS. You may make progress, but you'll likely encounter detours, wrong turns, and a sense of uncertainty. Similarly, embarking on your educational and career journey without self-discovery is akin to navigating life without a roadmap. Self-discovery serves as your compass, helping you understand your unique traits, preferences, and aspirations, and guiding you toward choices that resonate with your authentic self.

Why Self-Discovery Matters:

Alignment with Passion: Aligning your educational and career choices with your genuine passion is a powerful approach that can lead to a more fulfilling and successful life. When you know what truly excites you, your educational and career choices can be driven by genuine passion rather than external pressures or expectations. Passion serves as a powerful source of intrinsic motivation. You are driven by your inner desire to excel in your chosen field because you genuinely love what you're doing, rather than being motivated solely by external rewards like money or status. This intrinsic motivation often leads to better performance and greater perseverance in the face of challenges. Passion fuels a natural curiosity and desire for continuous learning. When you're passionate about a subject or career, you are more likely to seek out opportunities to expand your knowledge and skills voluntarily. This self-driven learning can lead to becoming an expert in your field over time. Pursuing your passion can help you develop resilience. You are more willing to overcome obstacles and setbacks because your passion provides you with the drive to keep pushing forward. Your love for what you do can help you bounce back from failures and setbacks more effectively.

In summary, aligning your educational and career choices with genuine passion empowers you to lead a more fulfilling, purpose-driven life. It can enhance your motivation, creativity, resilience, and overall well-being while also contributing positively to your personal growth and the greater community.

Enhanced decision-making through self-awareness means you can make choices that resonate with your core values, leverage your unique strengths, and lead you toward your desired long-term objectives. This self-understanding helps you avoid decisions driven by external pressures or societal expectations, ultimately leading to a more authentic and fulfilling life path.

Personal Fulfillment: Understanding yourself allows you to pursue paths that bring personal fulfillment, increasing your overall satisfaction with life.When you pursue something you are genuinely passionate about, it brings a sense of personal fulfillment and happiness. You wake up excited to tackle the challenges and tasks related to your education or career because they align with your interests and values.

Resilience: Self-discovery equips you with the self-awareness needed to navigate challenges, setbacks, and changes in your journey effectively. Pursuing your passion can help you develop resilience. You are more willing to overcome obstacles and setbacks because your passion provides you with the drive to keep pushing forward. Your love for what you do can help you bounce back from failures and setbacks more effectively.

Now, let's explore the components of self-discovery and how they can shape your educational and career path through real-life examples so that i can convey more effectively and you got the correc t message what i wanted to say beacuse these are very impoartant points.

1. Discovering Your Interests

Interests are the things that capture your attention, ignite your curiosity, and make you feel enthusiastic. They can be broad, such as a love for art or science, or more specific, like an interest in astrophysics or wildlife photography.

Example: Meet Priya, a young student with a strong interest in environmental conservation. She discovered this passion during a school project where she researched the impact of deforestation on local ecosystems. Priya's keen interest in environmental issues led her to explore careers in environmental science and conservation.

Action Steps for Exploring Interests:

Try New Activities: Experiment with various hobbies, sports, or extracurricular activities to identify what truly excites you.

Reflect: Journal about the activities that bring you joy and fulfillment.

Seek Guidance: Talk to mentors, teachers, or career counselors who can help you explore your interests further. Taking guidance is the most critical step beacuse only the experience peron can explain each and every thing to you.

2. Recognizing Your Strengths

Strengths are your innate talents, skills, and abilities. They are the areas where you naturally excel and feel confident. Recognizing your strengths can guide you toward careers where you can thrive.

Example: Consider Rahul, who always had an aptitude for mathematics and problem-solving. His teachers and parents recognized his talent and encouraged him to explore engineering as a potential career path. Today, Rahul is a successful civil engineer, using his strengths to design and build structures that improve lives.

Action Steps for Recognizing Strengths:

Self-Assessment: Take strengths assessments or quizzes to identify your natural talents. for example in Maths you have to divide the problem level wise so that you can judge your potential.

Feedback: Ask friends, family, and teachers for input on your strengths.

Skills Development: Cultivate and refine your strengths through education and practice. Always remeber practice makes a man perfect.

3. Understanding Your Values

Values are your deeply held beliefs and principles. They define what matters most to you in life and guide your decision-making. Understanding your values can help you align your education and career choices with what truly resonates with your heart and soul.

Example: Meet Anika, a humanitarian at heart. She values compassion, equality, and social justice. This led her to pursue a degree in social work, where she can make a positive impact on the lives of disadvantaged individuals and communities.

Action Steps for Understanding Values:

Reflect: Take time to consider the principles and beliefs that are most important to you.

Prioritize: Rank your values in order of importance to help you make choices that align with them.

Seek Opportunities: Look for educational and career paths that align with your core values.

4. Exploring Your Personality Traits

Personality traits encompass your unique characteristics, tendencies, and preferences. Understanding your personality can guide you toward environments and roles that suit your temperament.

Example: Imagine Sam, an introverted individual who thrives in quiet, reflective settings. Recognizing his personality traits, he pursued a career in research, allowing him to delve deep into his work, conduct experiments, and make valuable discoveries.

Action Steps for Exploring Personality Traits:

Self-Assessment: Take personality assessments like the Myers-Briggs Type Indicator (MBTI) or the Big Five Personality Test.

Observation: Reflect on how you respond to different situations and environments.

Seek Guidance: Consult with professionals who can provide insights into career paths that align with your personality.

5. Identifying Your Long-Term Goals

Long-term goals are the aspirations that guide your life choices over an extended period. They provide a sense of purpose and direction, shaping your educational and career trajectory.

Example: Meet Raj, a student with a long-term goal of improving healthcare access in rural communities. This goal motivated him to pursue a degree in medicine, with the aim of working in underserved areas and making a lasting impact on public health.

Action Steps for Identifying Long-Term Goals:

Visioning: Imagine where you see yourself in 5, 10, or 20 years.

Set Milestones: Break down your long-term goals into smaller, achievable milestones.

Plan Strategically: Create a plan that outlines the steps you need to take to reach your long-term goals.

The Intersection of Self-Discovery and Stream Selection

Now that we've explored the components of self-discovery, let's consider how this process intersects with the critical decision of selecting an academic stream. Your interests, strengths, values, personality traits, and long-term goals should all play a pivotal role in determining the most suitable stream for you.

For instance, if your self-discovery journey reveals a deep interest in biology, strengths in analytical thinking, a value for improving healthcare, and a long-term goal of becoming a medical researcher, it is likely that a science-oriented stream will be the most aligned choice for you. On the other hand, if you discover a passion for business and entrepreneurship, a commerce stream might better suit your aspirations.

Real-Life Success Story: Steve Jobs

Steve Jobs, co-founder of Apple Inc., is a remarkable example of how self-discovery can shape one's career path. In his early life, Jobs was passionate about technology and design. He dropped out of college to explore his interests in calligraphy and Eastern philosophy. These experiences shaped his unique approach to product design, which ultimately led to the creation of groundbreaking products like the iPhone and Macintosh.

Jobs' self-discovery journey, driven by his interests, values, and personality, played a pivotal role in his success. His story underscores the importance of following one's passion and values, even when it diverges from conventional educational and career paths.

Conclusion: Your Journey of Self-Discovery

As you embark on your journey of self-discovery, remember that it is an ongoing process. Your interests may evolve, your strengths may develop, and your values may deepen over time. Embrace change, be open to new experiences, and continually assess your alignment with your evolving self.

Self-discovery is not a destination but a lifelong quest. It is the compass that will guide you toward educational and career choices that resonate with your true self. By understanding your interests, recognizing your strengths, aligning with your values, embracing your personality traits, and identifying your long-term goals, you can navigate the intricate path of stream selection with clarity and confidence.

In the chapters that follow, we will explore each academic stream in-depth, offering insights into the subjects, career prospects, and skills required. Armed with the knowledge of self-discovery, you will be better equipped to make informed decisions about the most suitable stream for your unique journey.

Stay curious, stay true to yourself, and remember that the power of self-discovery lies within you. So, just give your best and wait for the rest..

This chapter provides an in-depth exploration of the importance of self-discovery and its role in shaping educational and career choices, offering real-life examples to illustrate key concepts.

CHAPTER FOUR

Navigating the Streams: Exploring Your Academic Options

In the previous chapter, "Discovering Your Path: The Power of Self-Exploration," we embarked on a transformative journey of self-discovery, exploring the importance of understanding your interests, strengths, values, personality traits, and long-term goals. This journey serves as the foundation for the chapter ahead, where we will continue our exploration of academic streams. Each stream represents a potential pathway, and by aligning your newfound self-awareness with these options, you can make a well-informed choice that resonates with your unique identity and aspirations. So, let's bridge the gap between self-discovery and stream selection as we dive into Chapter 4, "Navigating the Streams: Exploring Your Academic Options.

"As you stand at the crossroads of your academic journey after Class 10, one of the most significant decisions you'll make is selecting the right stream. Each stream represents a unique pathway, with its own set of subjects, career opportunities, and potential for personal growth. In this chapter, we will embark on a journey to explore the four main academic streams available to you in India: Science, Commerce, Arts, and Vocational. By understanding the nuances of each stream, you can make an informed decision that aligns with your interests, strengths, and aspirations.

1. Science Stream: Unleashing the Power of Discovery

The Science stream is often associated with a deep curiosity about the natural world and a desire to understand its mysteries. It offers a foundation in subjects like Physics, Chemistry, Biology, and Mathematics. If you have a passion for exploration, problem-solving, and a strong aptitude for quantitative thinking, the Science stream might be your ideal choice.

Subjects in Science Stream:

- Physics
- Chemistry
- Biology/Mathematics
- Optional Elective Subjects (e.g., Computer Science, Biotechnology etc)

Career Prospects:

- Medicine: Becoming a doctor or specialist
- Engineering: Pursuing various engineering disciplines
- Research: Contributing to scientific discoveries
- Information Technology: Entering the world of coding and software development
- Environmental Science: Focusing on sustainability and conservation

Pathways:

- After Class 12, you can appear for competitive exams like NEET or JEE for admission to medical or engineering colleges.
- Pursue a Bachelor's degree in your chosen field, followed by specialized Master's or Ph.D. programs.

- Explore interdisciplinary fields like biotechnology or data science.

2. Commerce Stream: Navigating the World of Business and Finance

The Commerce stream is ideal for those interested in economics, business, finance, and entrepreneurship. It equips you with a solid foundation in subjects like Accounting, Economics, Business Studies, and Mathematics. If you have a knack for financial management, an interest in market dynamics, or dreams of starting your own business, Commerce might be the path for you.

Subjects in Commerce Stream:

- Accounting
- Economics
- Business Studies
- Mathematics/Informatics Practices

Career Prospects:

- Chartered Accountancy (CA)
- Company Secretary (CS)
- Cost and Management Accountancy (CMA)
- Banking and Finance
- Business Management
- Entrepreneurship

Pathways:

- Pursue a Bachelor of Commerce (B.Com) or Bachelor of Business Administration (BBA) degree.
- Opt for professional courses like CA, CS, or CMA for specialized careers.

- Gain work experience through internships or entry-level positions in finance or business.

3. Arts Stream: Exploring the World of Creativity and Expression

- The Arts stream is a haven for those with a creative flair, a love for literature, and a passion for the humanities. It encompasses subjects like Literature, History, Geography, Psychology, Political Science, and more. If you find joy in self-expression, critical thinking, and exploring the human experience, the Arts stream may be your calling.

Subjects in Arts Stream:

- Literature
- History
- Geography
- Psychology
- Political Science
- Sociology
- Economics

Career Prospects:

- Journalism and Mass Communication
- Creative Writing
- Teaching and Education
- Social Work
- Counseling and Psychology
- Public Administration
- Civil Services

Pathways:

- Pursue a Bachelor of Arts (B.A.) degree with a specialization in your chosen subject.
- Consider postgraduate studies in areas like journalism, psychology, or public administration.
- Build a portfolio or gain experience through internships in your field of interest.

4. Vocational Stream: Building Practical Skills for the Future

The Vocational stream is designed for students who prefer hands-on learning and want to acquire practical skills that can lead to immediate employment. It includes a wide range of courses in fields such as Hospitality, Tourism, Agriculture, Healthcare, and more. If you have a specific trade or profession in mind and want to start your career early, the Vocational stream offers practical training.

Subjects in Vocational Stream:

- Hotel Management
- Agriculture
- Healthcare
- Information Technology
- Fashion Designing
- Automobile Mechanics
- Retail Management

Career Prospects:

- Hotel and Hospitality Industry
- Agriculture and Farming
- Paramedical Services
- Information Technology
- Fashion and Apparel Designing

- Automotive Industry
- Retail Management

Pathways:

- Enroll in vocational courses at the 10+2 level.
- Complete internships or apprenticeships in your chosen field.
- Pursue higher education or certification programs to enhance your skills and career prospects.

This chapter provides detailed information about the four main academic streams in India, offering insights into their subjects, career prospects, and potential pathways, while also encouraging students to consider their own interests, strengths, and goals in making a choice.

CHAPTER FIVE

Setting Your Course: Defining Educational and Career Goals

As you venture further into your educational journey, having a sense of direction becomes increasingly crucial. Chapter 4 introduced you to the various academic streams, helping you explore your options and interests. Now, it's time to take the next significant step: setting clear and meaningful educational and career goals within your chosen stream.

In this chapter, we will delve into the art of goal-setting and how it can shape your path within your selected academic stream. Goals act as guiding stars, providing you with a sense of purpose, motivation, and a roadmap to success. Whether you are pursuing Science, Commerce, Arts, or a Vocational stream, the principles of effective goal-setting remain universally applicable.

Why Set Goals? The Power of Direction

Imagine embarking on a journey without a destination in mind. While the journey itself can be enjoyable, you may eventually find yourself feeling lost and unsure of where you're headed. Goals give you that destination, providing clarity and purpose to your actions. Here's why setting goals is essential:

Motivation: Goals provide a reason to strive and put in effort. They act as motivators, driving you to overcome challenges and persevere.

Focus: When you have clear goals, it's easier to concentrate your efforts on tasks that align with your objectives, reducing distractions.

Measurement: Goals allow you to measure your progress and assess whether you're moving in the right direction.

Accountability: With set goals, you hold yourself accountable for your actions and outcomes.

Achievement: Accomplishing goals brings a sense of fulfillment and accomplishment, boosting self-esteem and confidence.

Types of Goals: Short-Term, Medium-Term, Long-Term

Goals can vary in terms of their timeframe and scope. Understanding the different types of goals will help you create a well-rounded plan for your academic and career journey.

1. Short-Term Goals: These are typically achievable within days, weeks, or a few months. They serve as stepping stones toward more significant objectives.

Example: Completing a specific project, improving grades in a particular subject, or mastering a specific skill.

2. Medium-Term Goals: These goals span a few months to a year or two. They require sustained effort and may involve multiple steps.

Example: Securing an internship, achieving a certain score in competitive exams, or completing a substantial coursework project.

3. Long-Term Goals: These are your overarching aspirations that can take several years to achieve. They define your ultimate purpose and guide your major life decisions.

Example: Earning a professional degree, establishing a successful career, or making a significant impact in your chosen field.

Creating Your Academic and Career Roadmap

Now, let's explore how to create a roadmap for setting and achieving your educational and career goals within your chosen stream:

1. Self-Reflection:

Before setting goals, reflect on your interests, strengths, values, and long-term aspirations within your academic stream.

Consider your passions, the subjects you excel in, and the kind of impact you wish to make in your chosen field.

2. Define Your Goals:

Start with your long-term goals. What major accomplishments do you hope to achieve within your chosen stream?

Break down your long-term goals into medium-term goals that you can achieve in the next few years.

Then, identify short-term goals that align with your medium-term objectives.

3. Specific and Measurable:

Ensure your goals are specific and measurable. Instead of a vague goal like "do well in exams," specify "score above 90% in the upcoming physics exam."

4. Achievable and Realistic:

Assess whether your goals are achievable and realistic given your resources, time, and abilities. Set yourself up for success, not overwhelm.

5. Time-Bound:

Assign deadlines to your goals. A timeframe creates a sense of urgency and helps you stay on track.

6. Written Goals:

Write down your goals. The act of writing makes your commitment tangible and reinforces your dedication to achieving them.

7. Plan of Action:

Outline the steps you need to take to accomplish each goal. What actions, resources, and support do you require?

8. Review and Adjust:

Periodically review your goals and assess your progress. Be willing to adjust your goals if circumstances change.

Real-Life Success Story: Kalpana Chawla

Kalpana Chawla, an Indian-American astronaut, serves as a remarkable example of the power of setting and achieving ambitious goals. As a young girl growing up in India, Kalpana dreamed of reaching the stars. Her goal was to become an astronaut, a dream that seemed out of reach for someone from a small town.

However, through unwavering determination, hard work, and a clear vision, Kalpana pursued her dream. She earned a degree in aerospace engineering, later obtaining a Ph.D. in the same field. Despite facing setbacks and challenges, she ultimately achieved her long-term goal by becoming the first woman of Indian origin in space.

Kalpana's story reminds us that even the most audacious dreams are attainable when backed by clear goals, determination, and a well-defined path.

Conclusion: Your Goals, Your Journey

In this chapter, we've explored the significance of goal-setting and how it can shape your educational and career journey within your chosen academic stream. Goals provide direction, motivation, and a sense of purpose as you navigate the complexities of your stream.

As you define your educational and career goals, remember that they are personal to you. Your goals should reflect your unique interests, strengths, and aspirations within your academic stream. With a well-thought-out roadmap and a commitment to your goals, you'll be better prepared to overcome challenges and seize opportunities that come your way.

In the upcoming chapters, we will delve deeper into each academic stream, offering insights and guidance to help you excel in your chosen field. Your journey has just begun, and each goal you set brings you one step closer to realizing your dreams within your selected stream.

So, set your course, embrace your goals, and embark on your path with confidence and determination. Your future within your chosen stream awaits, and the possibilities are endless.

This chapter provides detailed guidance on the importance of goal-setting within the chosen academic stream, offering insights into different types of goals, practical tips on creating a roadmap, and real-life success stories to inspire readers to set and achieve their goals.

CHAPTER SIX

Time Mastery: Efficient Study Habits for Stream Success

In the previous chapter, "Setting Your Course: Defining Educational and Career Goals," you laid the foundation for your academic and career journey within your chosen stream. You defined your goals, both short-term and long-term, and established a roadmap for success. Now, as we delve into Chapter 6, "Time Mastery: Efficient Study Habits for Stream Success," we will build upon those goals. Time management and effective study habits are the tools that will help you reach those milestones you've set. Just as a well-constructed bridge connects two shores, your goals and effective time management are the links between your aspirations and accomplishments. Let's explore how to build upon your goals with efficient time mastery and study habits.

Time is a precious resource, especially when it comes to excelling in your chosen academic stream. In this chapter, we will explore the art of time management and effective study habits, essential tools for your journey of success within your selected stream. Whether you're pursuing Science, Commerce, Arts, or a Vocational stream, mastering your time and study habits can make all the difference.

The Value of Time Management

Imagine you have a day filled with academic commitments, from classes and assignments to exams and extracurricular activities. Without effective time management, you might find yourself overwhelmed and struggling to meet deadlines. Time management is about making the most of your available time to maximize productivity and achieve your goals.

The Pomodoro Technique:

Let's start with an example of a popular time management technique called the Pomodoro Technique. This technique involves breaking your study time into focused intervals, typically 25 minutes each (known as "Pomodoros"), followed by a 5-minute break. After completing four Pomodoros, take a longer break of 15-30 minutes.

Example: Suppose you have a Physics chapter to study I have taken Physics here because physics is very intresting for me although I am a maths Faculty. Now, You decide to use the Pomodoro Technique. You set a timer for 25 minutes and study the chapter intensely. Once the timer rings, you take a 5-minute break to relax or stretch. After four Pomodoros, you reward yourself with a longer break, perhaps by going for a quick walk or having a snack, or you can play cricket i always advice students to play outdoor games never use mobile phone for games it will kill your creativity.

Rather that using mobile phones its better to have a conversation with your family and friends. In now a days it is very difficult still try to follow my request.

Effective Study Habits

Study habits play a significant role in how well you retain information and perform in exams. Here are some effective study habits that can help you succeed within your chosen stream:

1. Active Learning:

Instead of passively reading or listening to lectures, engage with the material actively. Take notes, ask questions, and discuss topics with peers. you should ask your doubt to your teacher without any hesitation. Also, I believe that Teachers should always be remembered for their willingness to welcome and embrace students' doubts and questions. They should never be judged based on the inquiries raised, as a true educator finds joy in addressing these doubts. It's important to focus on the value of learning and not be concerned with what others may think.

Example: In your maths class, when learning about Quadratic equation, create your own real-life based problem. This active engagement enhances your understanding.

2. Time Blocking:

Allocate specific blocks of time for different subjects or tasks. This helps you stay organized and ensures that you give each subject the attention it deserves. Most of the times students pay more attention to the topic or subject in which they are comfortable and skip the topic in which they are facing problem. Its my advice advice to you that you have to devote more time to the topic in ehich you are facing problem. Also, if possible write your weaker area and devote more time on it.

Example: Designate the morning hours for Science subjects, the afternoon for Commerce-related studies, and the evening for Arts assignments.

3. Use of Visual Aids:

Visual aids like mind maps, charts, and diagrams play a crucial role in enhancing the understanding of intricate subjects and bolstering memory retention. These graphical representations condense information into easily digestible formats, making it easier for individuals to grasp complex concepts. By engaging both visual and spatial memory, they help reinforce learning, making it more likely that the information will be retained and recalled effectively. In educational settings and professional presentations, the use of such visual aids proves valuable in conveying information clearly and promoting better comprehension.

Example: When studying Geography in the Arts stream, create a visual map of the world's major rivers and their tributaries. This makes the information more digestible.

4. Practice Problem Solving:

For subjects that involve problem-solving for example Maths, practice is key. Solve problems, exercises, and past exam papers to reinforce your understanding. Also develop a smart strategy let say you have solve 200 problem of straight line and in which 160 question you have solve easily and in rest 40 question you are having doubt then identify the topic on which those question based then revise the topic and then again solve the same question dont search the solution from internet it will kill your problem solving skill.

Example: In the Maths, if you're learning calculus, regularly solve calculus problems to hone your skills.As you know calculus is on of the difficult branch of mathematics.

5. Revision and Spaced Learning:

Regularly revise previously learned material to reinforce memory. Spaced learning involves reviewing information at intervals to enhance long-term retention.

Example: In Commerce, when studying accounting principles, review previously covered concepts each week to prevent forgetting and build a strong foundation.

6. Seek Clarity:

If you encounter challenging topics, don't hesitate to seek help from teachers, classmates. Here also i advice you can take refrence from internet but dont dependent on it beacuse it will consume your time you will see one video then another then some reels so it better that you can read books.

Example: In the Vocational stream, if you're learning about healthcare procedures and find a specific technique confusing, consult your faculty.

Real-Life Success Story: Elon Musk

Elon Musk, the visionary entrepreneur behind SpaceX and Tesla, demonstrates the power of effective time management and study habits. As a young student, Musk devoured books on various subjects, often reading for hours each day. His habit of continuous learning and focused study helped him become a visionary leader in the fields of space exploration and electric vehicles.

Musk's story reminds us that success is not solely about innate talent but also about how effectively you manage your time and apply yourself to learning and problem-solving.

Conclusion: Mastering Your Time and Study Habits

In this chapter, we've explored the importance of time management and effective study habits for success within your chosen academic stream. Whether you're studying Science, Commerce, Arts, or a Vocational stream, these tools can significantly impact your performance and overall well-being.

Remember, time management is about making the most of your time, and effective study habits are about optimizing your learning process. By implementing techniques like the Pomodoro Technique, active learning, time blocking, visual aids, and regular revision, you can enhance your study experience and achieve your goals.

As you progress in your educational journey, continue to refine your time management skills and study habits. Your ability to manage your time efficiently and learn effectively will not only help you excel academically but also contribute to your growth as a well-rounded individual within your chosen stream.

In the upcoming chapters, we'll delve deeper into stream-specific strategies and insights to help you navigate the unique challenges and opportunities within your academic field. With strong time management and study habits as your foundation, you're well-equipped to thrive in your chosen stream.

So, embrace the power of time mastery and effective study habits as you continue your journey of stream success.

This chapter provides detailed guidance on time management and effective study habits, including practical examples and real-life success stories to illustrate key concepts. It empowers students with the tools they need to excel in their chosen academic stream.

CHAPTER SEVEN

Some National Level Exams

In this chapter I am providing a comprehensive list of most of national level exams in India and a approximate number of candidates sitting for each of them so that you will get an idea of competition, it will also help you to plan your academic journey.

1. Joint Entrance Examination (JEE) Main

- **Purpose**: For admission to various engineering colleges in India.
- **Candidates**: Approximately 9 to 12 lakh candidates annually.

2. National Eligibility cum Entrance Test (NEET)

- **Purpose**: For admission to undergraduate medical and dental courses.
- **Candidates**: Around 15 to 16 lakh candidates.

3. Union Public Service Commission (UPSC) Civil Services Examination

- **Purpose**: For recruitment to various Civil Services of the Government of India.
- **Candidates**: Nearly 10 lakh candidates, with around 5 lakh candidates actually appearing for the exam.

4. Common Admission Test (CAT)

- **Purpose**: For admission to management programs in IIMs and other leading B-schools.
- **Candidates**: About 2 to 2.5 lakh candidates annually.

5. Graduate Aptitude Test in Engineering (GATE)

- **Purpose**: For admission to postgraduate engineering programs and PSU recruitment.
- **Candidates**: Approximately 8 to 9 lakh candidates.

6. Central Teacher Eligibility Test (CTET)

- **Purpose**: Qualification exam for teachers for classes I to VIII.
- **Candidates**: Around 14 to 16 lakh candidates.

7. Staff Selection Commission (SSC) Combined Graduate Level Examination (CGL)

- **Purpose:** For recruitment to various posts in ministries, departments, and organizations of the Government of India.
- **Candidates:** Roughly 15 to 30 lakh candidates.

8. Institute of Banking Personnel Selection (IBPS) PO Exam

- **Purpose:** For recruitment of Probationary Officers in various public sector banks.
- **Candidates:** Approximately 10 to 20 lakh candidates.

9. National Defence Academy (NDA) and Naval Academy Examination

- **Purpose:** For admission to the Army, Navy, and Air Force wings of the NDA.
- **Candidates:** Around 4 to 6 lakh candidates.

10. Common Law Admission Test (CLAT)

- **Purpose:** For admission to undergraduate and postgraduate law programs.
- **Candidates:** Approximately 50,000 to 60,000 candidates.

Note:

- The number of candidates can vary year to year based on several factors including the exam's popularity, changes in eligibility criteria, and the overall job market scenario.
- These figures are based on general trends and should be verified with the latest data for specific years.

CHAPTER EIGHT

Career Options

In this chapter we are going to discuss career options in diffrent "STREAM"

Science Stream - Medical Science Career Options:

- MBBS, BDS (Dentistry), BAMS (Ayurveda), BHMS (Homeopathy)
- BPT (Physiotherapy), B.Sc Nursing, B.Pharm (Pharmacy)
- Medical Researcher
- Nutritionist/Dietician
- Paramedical Services (like Medical Lab Technician)
- Public Health Administrator
- Veterinary Doctor.

Reasons for Choosing This Stream:

- Interest in biological sciences
- Desire to work in healthcare or medical research
- Passion for helping and treating people
- Interest in veterinary science

Science Stream - Non-Medical Science/Engineering Career Options:

- Engineering
- Environmental Scientist
- Forensic Scientist
- Astrophysicist
- Geologist
- Biotechnologist
- Statistician
- Robotics Engineer

Reasons for Choosing This Stream:

- Strong interest in mathematics and physical sciences
- Curiosity about how things work
- Fascination with space, environment, or technology
- Drive towards innovation and problem-solving

Commerce Stream Career Options:

- Entrepreneur
- Investment Banker
- Tax Consultant
- Human Resources Manager
- Insurance Broker
- Retail Manager
- Market Research Analyst

Reasons for Choosing This Stream:

- Interest in business and finance
- Ambition to start a business
- Knack for numbers and economics
- Career aspirations in corporate sectors
- Interest in management and organizational dynamics

Arts/Humanities Stream Career Options:

- Graphic Designer
- Content Writer/Editor
- Sociologist
- Archaeologist
- International Relations Specialist
- Public Relations Officer
- Translator/Interpreter
- Event Planner

Reasons for Choosing This Stream:

- Strong inclination towards arts, languages, history, or social sciences
- Creative and critical thinking skills
- Interest in understanding human behavior and societal dynamics
- Passion for writing and communication

Vocational Stream Career Options:

- IT and Network Specialist
- Automotive Technician
- Multimedia Artist
- Healthcare Assistant
- Renewable Energy Technician
- Fashion Merchandiser
- Agricultural Technician

Reasons for Choosing This Stream:

- Desire for skill-based education
- Preference for hands-on learning
- Interest in specific trades or technical fields
- Aim to enter the workforce earlier
- Inclination towards a practical approach in education

Each stream leads to a variety of higher education options and career paths. The choice of stream should be based on the student's interests, strengths, and career goals.

Here I am going to provide some information about the number of Indian Institutes of Technology (IITs) and National Institutes of Technology (NITs) in India, along with an overview of the available seats

Indian Institutes of Technology (IITs)

Number of IITs: There are 23 IITs in India.

Total Seats: The total number of seats in IITs varies each year, with fluctuations based on new courses introduced, seat reservations, and other factors. As of the most recent data, there are approximately 16,000 seats across all IITs. However, this number is subject to change annually.

National Institutes of Technology (NITs)

Number of NITs: There are 31 NITs in India.

Total Seats: Similar to the IITs, the total number of seats in NITs also varies annually. As of the latest information, there are approximately 20,000 seats across all NITs. Again, this number is subject to change each year.

Admission and Seat Allocation

- Admission Process: Admission to both IITs and NITs is primarily through the Joint Entrance Examination (JEE), with JEE Main being the qualifying exam for NITs and the first stage for IITs. The JEE Advanced is required for admission into the IITs.
- Seat Reservation: Both IITs and NITs have seat reservations based on government policies, including reservations for SC, ST, OBC, EWS, and PwD candidates.

JEE Exams and Cutoffs

- JEE Mains and Advanced: The Joint Entrance Examination (JEE) is conducted in two phases - JEE Mains and JEE Advanced. JEE Mains is the preliminary phase and a qualifying exam for JEE Advanced, which is required for admission to the IITs.
- Cutoffs: The cutoffs for these exams vary each year and depend on various factors like the difficulty level of the exam, number of candidates appearing, and the number of seats available. Cutoffs

are generally category-specific (General, OBC-NCL, SC, ST, EWS, etc.).

- Number of Students: The number of students appearing for JEE Mains is usually in the range of 9 to 11 lakh annually. For JEE Advanced, only the top candidates from JEE Mains (around 2.5 lakh) are eligible to appear.

Note: The exact number of seats available can vary each year due to the introduction of new programs, changes in reservation policies, and other institutional decisions

Average Package After Completing BTech from IIT

Average Salary Package: The average salary package for BTech graduates from IITs varies widely based on the specialization, industry demand, and the economic climate. As of the last few years, the average package generally ranges between INR 10 to 20 Lakh per annum. However, for top branches like Computer Science and Engineering, the average package can be significantly higher.

Placement Records: IITs have excellent placement records, with many students receiving offers from top global and Indian companies. Placement seasons often witness participation from a mix of technology firms, consultancies, and core engineering companies.

Eminent Personalities Who Are IIT Alumni

- **Sundar Pichai**: CEO of Alphabet Inc. and its subsidiary Google LLC. He graduated from IIT Kharagpur with a degree in Metallurgical Engineering.
- **N. R. Narayana Murthy**: Co-founder of Infosys, one of India's largest IT companies. He studied Electrical Engineering at IIT Kanpur.
- **Arun Sarin**: Former CEO of Vodafone Group. He completed his BTech in Metallurgical Engineering from IIT Kharagpur.
- **Raghuram Rajan**: Former Governor of the Reserve Bank of India and a notable economist. He is an alumnus of IIT Delhi.

- **Nikesh Arora**: Former President and COO of SoftBank Group, previously a senior executive at Google. He holds a BTech degree from IIT Varanasi (formerly BHU).
- **Chetan Bhagat**: Chetan Bhagat is an alumnus of IIT Delhi, where he completed his degree in Mechanical Engineering.

Career Shift: Despite his technical background, Chetan Bhagat pursued a career in writing and has become one of the most popular and best-selling authors in India.

Manohar Parrikar

Background: Manohar Parrikar was an alumnus of IIT Bombay, where he completed his degree in Metallurgical Engineering.

Career Path: He entered politics and became a prominent figure in Indian politics. Parrikar served as the Chief Minister of Goa and was also the Defence Minister of India.

Contributions: Known for his simplicity and efficient administrative skills, he played a crucial role in formulating defense policies for India.

Nandan Nilekani

Background: Nandan Nilekani graduated from IIT Bombay with a degree in Electrical Engineering.

Diverse Roles: While he started his career in technology, co-founding Infosys, Nilekani later took on roles that intersected technology, business, and public policy.

Public Service: He chaired the Unique Identification Authority of India (UIDAI), the agency overseeing the Aadhaar project, which is the world's largest biometric ID system.

Arvind Kejriwal

Background: Arvind Kejriwal completed his Mechanical Engineering degree from IIT Kharagpur.

Shift to Civil Services and Politics: Initially working in the Indian Revenue Service, he later ventured into social activism and politics.

Political Career: He is the founder of the Aam Aadmi Party (AAP) and has served as the Chief Minister of Delhi.

Raghuram Rajan

Background: Although mentioned earlier, Raghuram Rajan, an alumnus of IIT Delhi, deserves another mention for his exceptional contribution in economics.

Economics and Academia: After IIT, he pursued a doctoral degree in management from the Massachusetts Institute of Technology (MIT). Rajan has served as the Chief Economist at the International Monetary Fund (IMF) and the Governor of the Reserve Bank of India (RBI).

Contributions: He is renowned for his analysis of financial crises and was among the few who warned about the 2008 financial crisis.

These individuals showcase the diverse paths IIT alumni have taken, contributing significantly to various sectors such as politics, public administration, economics, and literature. Their careers illustrate that an IIT education provides a strong foundation, enabling graduates to excel in a broad range of fields.

Eminent Persons from Different Streams other than Science

Commerce Stream

- **Indra Nooyi**: Former CEO of PepsiCo. She studied Bachelor's degree in Physics, Chemistry and Mathematics, followed by a Post-Graduate Programme (MBA) from Indian Institute of

Management Calcutta.

- **Kumar Mangalam Birla**: Chairman of the Aditya Birla Group. He holds a Bachelor of Commerce degree and an MBA from London Business School.

Arts/Humanities Stream

- **Amartya Sen**: Nobel laureate in Economics. He studied Economics at Presidency College in Kolkata, a course that falls under the Arts stream.
- **Shashi Tharoor**: Indian politician and former international diplomat. He has a Bachelor of Arts in History.

Vocational Stream

- **Ritesh Agarwal**: Founder and CEO of OYO Rooms, a successful hospitality business. He dropped out of college to pursue his business dreams, but his initial education was in a vocational stream focusing on coding and software development.

Individuals Who Opted for a Different Career

Commerce Stream

- **Chanda Kochhar**: Former MD and CEO of ICICI Bank. She began her career in management and later shifted to banking.

Arts/Humanities Stream

- **Satyajit Ray**: A renowned filmmaker and writer. He studied at a fine arts college but became famous for his work in cinema.

Vocational Stream

- **George Lucas**: The creator of "Star Wars." He studied cinematography, a vocational subject, and became a filmmaker.

Average Package of Different Streams

Commerce Stream

- **Average Salary**: For fresh graduates, it ranges from INR 3 to 6 Lakh per annum. For those who complete professional courses like CA or MBA, it can be significantly higher.

Arts/Humanities Stream

- **Average Salary**: It varies widely based on the specific field. For example, in fields like media, journalism, and content creation, the starting salary can range from INR 2.5 to 5 Lakh per annum. In more specialized roles like economists or psychologists, the package can be higher.

Vocational Stream

- **Average Salary**: This also varies greatly depending on the trade. For example, in fields like hospitality management or multimedia arts, the starting salary can range from INR 3 to 8 Lakh per annum.

Note:

The salaries mentioned are approximate and can vary based on various factors such as the college's prestige, the student's skill set, the industry's demand, and the geographical location of the job. Also, the individuals listed as examples have had diverse career paths and their current status might not directly reflect their initial educational background.

CHAPTER NINE

Jobs

In this chapter we are going to get an idea of current trending jobs and future trending jobs in diffrent stream that will provide you more clearity to select a Stream of your choice.

CURRENT

1. Science Stream

Current Trending Jobs

- **Data Scientist / Data Analyst**: With the explosion of data in every sector, there is a high demand for professionals who can interpret complex data sets to drive strategic decision-making.
- **Cybersecurity Specialist**: As cyber threats increase, organizations are investing heavily in securing their data and systems, leading to a surge in demand for cybersecurity experts.
- **Healthcare Professionals (like Biomedical Engineers, Genetic Counselors)**: Advances in medical technology and an aging population have led to a growing need for specialized healthcare services.

Reasons for Popularity

- The digital transformation across industries has created a vast amount of data, necessitating skilled professionals to analyze it.
- Increasing cyber threats and data breaches make cybersecurity a critical aspect of every organization.
- Technological advances in healthcare and the ongoing global health challenges have highlighted the need for specialized healthcare professionals.

2. Commerce Stream

Current Trending Jobs

- **Financial Analyst / Investment Banker**: With the growing complexity of financial markets, there is a high demand for professionals who can analyze investments and financial strategies.
- **Digital Marketing Specialist**: The shift towards digital platforms has increased the need for experts in digital marketing strategies.
- **Accountants and Auditors with IT Knowledge**: The integration of accounting with IT systems (like ERP software) has created a demand for accountants who are also tech-savvy.

Reasons for Popularity

- The complexity and global nature of modern financial markets require sophisticated analysis and advisory roles.
- The shift in consumer behavior towards online platforms has made digital marketing critical for business growth.
- The use of technology in finance and accounting has transformed traditional roles, requiring a new set of skills.

3. Arts/Humanities Stream

Current Trending Jobs

- **User Experience (UX) / User Interface (UI) Designers**: As businesses focus on online presence, there's a high demand for designers who can create engaging and user-friendly digital experiences.
- **Content Creators and Social Media Managers**: The rise of social media and content platforms has created a demand for skilled content creators and social media strategists.
- **Mental Health Professionals**: Increasing awareness of mental health issues has led to a growing need for professionals in this field.

Reasons for Popularity

- The importance of digital interface design in customer satisfaction and business success is driving demand for UX/UI designers.
- The influence of digital and social media in marketing and public relations has made these roles essential.
- Growing societal awareness and acceptance of mental health issues have increased the need for qualified professionals.

4. Vocational Stream

Current Trending Jobs

- **Renewable Energy Technicians**: As the world moves towards sustainable energy sources, skilled technicians in this field are increasingly in demand.

- **IT and Network Support Specialists**: The reliance on technology in business and everyday life has created a constant need for IT support professionals.
- **Healthcare Technicians (such as Radiology Techs, Dental Hygienists)**: There's a growing need for healthcare technicians due to technological advancements in medicine and an aging population.

Reasons for Popularity

- The global shift towards renewable energy is driving demand for skilled technicians in this sector.
- The dependence on technology in all sectors creates a consistent need for IT support and maintenance.
- Advances in medical technology and an aging population require more specialized healthcare technicians.

These trends reflect how technological advancement, digital transformation, evolving market needs, and societal changes are shaping the job market. The popularity of these roles is largely driven by the intersection of these trends with the need for specialized skills and knowledge.

FUTURE

1. Science Stream

Future Career Trends

- **Biotechnology and Genetic Engineering**: With advancements in genetics, careers in gene editing, personalized medicine, and biotech research are expected to grow.
- **Environmental Science and Sustainability**: Roles focusing on climate change, renewable energy, and sustainable development

will become increasingly important.

- **Artificial Intelligence and Machine Learning**: Specialists in AI, robotics, and data science will be in high demand as these technologies continue to advance.
- **Neuroscience and Mental Health**: Increased focus on mental health and neurological research could lead to new career opportunities.

Reasons for Choosing

- A strong interest in scientific inquiry and research.
- Aspiration to contribute to major scientific breakthroughs or address global challenges like climate change.
- A desire to be at the forefront of technological and medical innovations.

2. Commerce Stream

Future Career Trends

- **Digital Finance and Fintech**: Careers in financial technology, blockchain, and cryptocurrency are emerging rapidly.
- **E-Commerce and Digital Marketing**: With the growth of online businesses, there will be a greater need for digital marketing and e-commerce specialists.
- **Sustainable Business Practices and CSR**: Roles focusing on corporate social responsibility and sustainable business models are gaining importance.
- **Data Analytics in Business**: The use of big data in decision-making processes in businesses is creating new opportunities.

Reasons for Choosing

- Interest in the dynamics of business, economics, and finance.

- Aim to pursue careers in the burgeoning fields of fintech, marketing, or entrepreneurship.
- Desire to understand and influence the economic and financial frameworks that drive the world.

3. Arts/Humanities Stream

Future Career Trends

- **Digital Humanities and Cultural Informatics**: Leveraging technology to study human culture and history.
- **Content Creation and New Media**: With the rise of digital media, there's growing demand for content creators, digital journalists, and social media influencers.
- **International Relations and Global Studies**: As the world becomes more interconnected, expertise in global politics and international relations will be crucial.
- **Community and Social Development**: Roles in NGOs, community development, and social work will continue to be vital.

Reasons for Choosing

- A passion for understanding diverse cultures, languages, history, and societal structures.
- Desire to impact society positively through social work, education, or cultural preservation.
- Interest in creative expression, storytelling, or influencing public opinion.

4. Vocational Stream

Future Career Trends

- **Renewable Energy Technology**: With the shift towards sustainable energy, careers in this sector are expected to grow.
- **Healthcare Technology and Telemedicine**: The integration of technology in healthcare will create new vocational roles.
- **Cybersecurity and IT Support**: As cybersecurity threats increase, skilled professionals in this area will be in high demand.
- **Creative Industries (like Gaming and VR)**: The entertainment and creative industries are rapidly evolving with new technologies.

Reasons for Choosing

- Interest in acquiring specific, hands-on skills that are directly applicable to a job.
- Desire for a quicker pathway to employment in industries that require specialized skills.
- Aiming to be part of innovative fields like renewable energy, healthcare technology, or digital arts.

The future of work is evolving, and these streams are adapting to prepare students for emerging careers. The choice of a stream is often driven by personal interests, skills, and the desire to engage in specific sectors of the economy or society.

Average Income in India

- **National Average**: The average annual income in India varies significantly across different regions and sectors. As of the latest reports, the average annual income was estimated to be around

INR 1,35,000 to INR 1,50,000. However, this is a very broad average and can be misleading as there is a large disparity in income levels across the country.

Sector-wise Average Income

1. **IT and Technology Sector**: One of the highest paying sectors, especially for skilled professionals. Average salaries can range from INR 4,00,000 to over INR 20,00,000 per annum for experienced professionals.
2. **Healthcare and Pharmaceutical Sector**: Doctors, specialists, and pharmaceutical professionals can earn substantially. On average, salaries can range from INR 3,00,000 to INR 12,00,000 per annum, increasing with specialization and experience.
3. **Finance and Banking Sector**: For roles in banking, finance, and accounting, the average salary can range from INR 2,50,000 to INR 10,00,000 per annum, with higher earnings potential in roles like investment banking.
4. **Engineering and Manufacturing Sector**: Engineers and manufacturing professionals can expect average salaries from INR 3,00,000 to INR 8,00,000 per annum, depending on the field of engineering and level of expertise.
5. **Education and Teaching Sector**: The average income in this sector can vary widely based on the institution and level of teaching. It typically ranges from INR 2,00,000 to INR 10,00,000 per annum.
6. **Agriculture Sector**: This sector often sees lower average incomes due to the nature of the industry and market fluctuations. Average incomes can be around INR 1,00,000 to INR 3,00,000 per annum.
7. **Retail and Hospitality Sector**: Salaries in these sectors can range from INR 1,80,000 to INR 5,00,000 per annum, varying greatly with position and experience.

8. **Construction and Real Estate Sector**: Incomes vary widely depending on the role, but on average can range from INR 2,00,000 to INR 7,00,000 per annum.

I am providing estimated average numbers for the number of jobs in major sectors in India. It's important to note that these numbers are approximations and are intended to give a general idea of the distribution of jobs across sectors.

Estimated Number of Jobs in Major Sectors in India

1. **IT and Technology Sector**: 10 million jobs
2. **Healthcare and Pharmaceutical Sector**: 5 million jobs
3. **Finance and Banking Sector**: 7 million jobs
4. **Engineering and Manufacturing Sector**: 15 million jobs
5. **Education and Teaching Sector**: 9 million jobs
6. **Agriculture Sector**: 150 million jobs
7. **Retail and Hospitality Sector**: 35 million jobs
8. **Construction and Real Estate Sector**: 50 million jobs

Note

- These figures are approximate and subject to change based on economic conditions, market demand, and other factors.
- The disparity in income across different regions and between urban and rural areas in India is significant.
- For the most current and detailed data, it's recommended to consult the latest reports from reliable sources such as government publications, industry reports, and economic surveys.

CHAPTER TEN

NEP

What is the New Education Policy (NEP)?

The NEP is a comprehensive framework to guide the development of education in India. It aims to make education more holistic, flexible, and aligned with the 21st-century needs. Here's a simple breakdown:

1. **Holistic Education**: Instead of focusing only on academic subjects, the NEP emphasizes overall development. This means students will learn not just math and science, but also skills like critical thinking, creativity, and ethics.
2. **Flexibility in Subject Choice**: Students can choose a mix of subjects across streams (like Science, Arts, and Commerce). For example, a student can study both physics and history together.
3. **Focus on Vocational Education**: Starting from a young age, students will be exposed to vocational education like carpentry, coding, etc. This is to ensure that they acquire practical skills along with academic knowledge.
4. **Multilingualism**: The NEP encourages teaching in the mother tongue or local language till at least Grade 5, to make education more accessible and effective.
5. **Continuous Assessment**: Instead of relying on board exams, the NEP suggests a more continuous and comprehensive evaluation to reduce stress on students.

How Does It Meet Current Needs and Help Compete Globally?

1. **Skill Development**: By focusing on skills like problem-solving and critical thinking, the NEP prepares students for modern challenges, making them ready for both local and global job markets.
2. **Flexibility and Choice**: The ability to choose subjects across streams helps nurture diverse talents and interests, creating individuals with broader skill sets.
3. **Practical Learning**: Emphasis on vocational training ensures that students not only learn theoretical concepts but also how to apply them in real-world situations.
4. **Inclusivity and Accessibility**: Teaching in local languages and continuous assessment makes education more inclusive and accessible to all, regardless of socio-economic backgrounds.
5. **Technology Integration**: The NEP promotes the use of technology in education, which is essential in today's digital world and helps students become globally competitive.

Why is it Required?

- **Changing Job Market**: The job market is evolving rapidly, and there's a need for people with diverse skills and innovative thinking.
- **Globalization**: As the world becomes more interconnected, education needs to prepare students to compete and collaborate on a global scale.
- **Technological Advancements**: With rapid advancements in technology, students need to be proficient in new tools and ways of thinking.

- **Social and Economic Challenges**: Education must address broader social and economic challenges, and empower students to be responsible and proactive citizens.

In summary, the NEP aims to transform the Indian education system to be more holistic, flexible, and in tune with the current times. It's designed to nurture critical thinking, creativity, and practical skills, preparing students to succeed in a rapidly changing world and contribute positively to society. Now lets understand it through some examples.

Example 1: Multidisciplinary Approach

Old System: Traditionally, students had to choose a specific stream (Science, Commerce, or Arts) after the 10th grade, and their subject choices were limited to that stream.

NEP Implementation: A student can now choose a combination of subjects across streams. For example, a student interested in both Physics (Science stream) and Economics (Commerce stream) can study them together.

Impact: This flexibility allows students to explore a broader range of subjects and develop a more rounded skill set, which is beneficial in a job market that values versatility and interdisciplinary knowledge.

Example 2: Vocational Education

Old System: Vocational education was often seen as a secondary option, mainly for students not pursuing higher academic studies.

NEP Implementation: Vocational training is integrated into the school curriculum from the 6th grade onwards, with options like coding, carpentry, electrical work, etc.

Impact: Early exposure to vocational skills can help students discover their aptitude and passion for practical subjects. This approach also elevates the importance of vocational education, leading to a workforce that is skilled in diverse areas.

Example 3: Focus on Local Languages

Old System: English and Hindi were predominantly used as mediums of instruction, which could be a barrier for students from regional backgrounds.

NEP Implementation: Emphasizing teaching in the mother tongue or regional languages up to the 5th grade (or beyond) helps make education more relatable and easier to grasp for many students.

Impact: This can lead to better understanding and retention of knowledge, especially in primary education, laying a stronger foundation for future learning.

Example 4: Technology Integration

Old System: Limited use of technology in teaching and learning, especially in rural and semi-urban areas.

NEP Implementation: Promotes the use of technology in education, including online learning tools and digital literacy.

Impact: This prepares students for a digital future and bridges the educational divide by providing access to quality learning resources across various regions.

Example 5: Continuous and Comprehensive Evaluation

Old System: Heavy emphasis on board exams and year-end tests, creating significant stress for students.

NEP Implementation: Suggests more regular and formative assessments to track student progress.

Impact: Reduces the pressure of final exams and encourages consistent learning and understanding throughout the year.

These examples illustrate how the NEP can make education more inclusive, practical, and aligned with the needs of a modern, diverse, and rapidly evolving society. The policy's success will largely depend on effective implementation and the collective effort of educators, policymakers, and communities.

CHAPTER ELEVEN

Role Of Parents

Parents play a pivotal role in their children's education. They serve as the first and most influential teachers, laying the foundation for learning and instilling essential values. Beyond providing a supportive and nurturing environment, parents can actively engage in their child's education by helping with homework, fostering a love for reading, and encouraging curiosity. They also play a vital role in shaping a child's attitudes towards education, setting high expectations, and offering guidance throughout their academic journey. Additionally, parents can collaborate with teachers and schools to ensure a holistic and successful educational experience for their children, promoting lifelong learning and personal growth.

Absolutely, the role of parents is crucial in guiding their children through the important decision of stream selection after Class 10. Here are some suggestions for parents:

1. Encourage Open Communication

- **Example**: Create an environment where your child feels comfortable discussing their interests, strengths, and fears. For instance, if your child shows a keen interest in creative writing or painting, discuss the potential of pursuing Arts without imposing preconceived notions about 'conventional' careers.
- **Advice**: Listen actively to your child's thoughts and aspirations. Understand that their interests and passions might differ from

your own or from traditional expectations.

2. Help Explore Different Options

- **Example**: If your child is uncertain, help them research various streams and career paths. Arrange meetings with educators or professionals in different fields, or attend career fairs together.
- **Advice**: Assist in gathering information about each stream, including subject combinations, future prospects, and aligning them with the child's interests and abilities.

3. Avoid Imposing Your Own Aspirations

- **Example**: Sometimes, parents might project their unfulfilled ambitions on their children. If you always wanted to be an engineer but your child is inclined towards Literature, support their preference.
- **Advice**: Recognize and respect your child's individuality and unique talents. The best outcomes occur when children are supported in pursuing their own passions.

4. Consider Professional Career Counseling

- **Example**: If making a decision becomes challenging.

Parents have to kept in mind that Students today face a variety of challenges, both academic and non-academic, in an increasingly complex and fast-paced world. Being aware of these hurdles is crucial for both parents and students to navigate them effectively.

Here are some key challenges and considerations:

1. Academic Pressure and Stress

- **For Students**: The pressure to perform well in exams and secure admission to prestigious institutions can be overwhelming.
- **For Parents**: Recognize the signs of stress and provide support. Encourage a balanced approach to studies and extracurricular activities.

2. Mental Health Concerns

- **For Students**: Issues like anxiety, depression, and stress are increasingly prevalent. It's important to seek help when needed.
- **For Parents**: Create an environment where mental health is openly discussed. Be supportive and consider professional help if necessary.

3. Digital Distractions and Screen Time

- **For Students**: Excessive use of digital devices and social media can lead to distractions, affecting academic performance and social skills.
- **For Parents**: Monitor and set reasonable limits on screen time. Encourage offline activities and hobbies.

4. Peer Pressure and Bullying

- **For Students:** Navigating social dynamics and peer influence, including negative aspects like bullying, can be challenging.
- **For Parents:** Keep communication lines open. Discuss issues like peer pressure and bullying, and be prepared to intervene if necessary.

5. Career Uncertainty

- **For Students:** Choosing a career path can be daunting, especially with the rapidly changing job market.
- **For Parents:** Guide them in exploring their interests and skills. Consider career counseling for informed decision-making.

6. Information Overload

- **For Students:** The vast amount of information available online can be overwhelming and sometimes misleading.
- **For Parents:** Teach critical thinking and how to discern credible sources of information.

7. Lack of Physical Activity

- **For Students:** A sedentary lifestyle can lead to health issues.
- **For Parents:** Encourage regular physical activity and participation in sports or outdoor activities.

8. Unrealistic Expectations

- **For Students**: Social media can create unrealistic expectations about life and success.
- **For Parents**: Encourage a realistic understanding of success and failure. Celebrate efforts and small victories.

9. Environmental and Societal Issues

- **For Students**: Concerns about global issues like climate change, inequality, and political unrest can cause anxiety.
- **For Parents**: Discuss these issues openly, focusing on positive actions and resilience.

10. Preparing for the Future

- **For Students**: The future requires adaptability, lifelong learning, and diverse skill sets.
- **For Parents**: Encourage learning beyond textbooks, including soft skills like communication, empathy, and problem-solving.

Conclusion

- **For Students**: It's important to balance academics with personal well-being and to cultivate a broad set of skills.
- **For Parents**: Support and guidance are crucial, but so is giving space for independence and self-exploration. Understanding and addressing these challenges together can lead to a more fulfilling and less stressful educational journey.

CHAPTER TWELVE

Social Media Impact and Solution

The advent of social media and the ubiquity of mobile devices have significantly transformed students' lives and learning experiences. While these technologies offer numerous educational benefits, they also present unique challenges, particularly in the realms of focus, mental health, and social interactions.

Impact on Student Life and Study

1. **Distraction and Reduced Concentration**

- **Description**: Constant notifications and the lure of social media can lead to fragmented attention spans, making it difficult for students to concentrate on their studies.
- **Example**: A student might find themselves checking their phone every few minutes while studying, significantly reducing effective study time.

2. Impact on Mental Health

- **Description**: Prolonged use of social media has been linked to increased rates of anxiety, depression, and low self-esteem among students, often due to cyberbullying or unrealistic comparisons with peers.

- **Example**: A student might feel inadequate or left out after seeing peers posting about achievements or social gatherings.

3. **Sleep Disruption**

   - **Description**: Excessive screen time, especially before bedtime, can interfere with sleep patterns, leading to fatigue and decreased academic performance.
   - **Example**: Using a phone late at night can hinder a student's ability to fall asleep, reducing their alertness the next day.

4. **Erosion of Social Skills**

   - **Description**: Overreliance on digital communication can impair the development of face-to-face interaction skills.
   - **Example**: A student who primarily interacts through text messages may struggle with verbal and non-verbal cues in in-person interactions.

Strategies to Mitigate Negative Impacts

1. **Setting Boundaries**

   - **Action**: Establish specific times for using social media and stick to a schedule to avoid constant distractions.
   - **Benefit**: Helps in cultivating self-discipline and improves focus during study sessions.

2. **Digital Detox**

   - **Action**: Regular intervals of disconnecting from digital devices, especially during family time and before bed.
   - **Benefit**: Enhances sleep quality and provides mental space for reflection and relaxation.

3. **Mindful Use of Technology**

    - **Action**: Being aware of the purpose and duration of each session of technology use.
    - **Benefit**: Prevents aimless browsing and encourages more productive use of time.

4. **Promoting Offline Interactions**

    - **Action**: Engaging in extracurricular activities, sports, and face-to-face gatherings.
    - **Benefit**: Develops interpersonal skills and provides a healthy balance between online and offline worlds.

5. **Educational Use of Technology**

    - **Action**: Leveraging technology for educational purposes, like research and learning new skills.
    - **Benefit**: Makes technology a tool for academic enhancement rather than a distraction.

Conclusion

While social media and mobile devices are integral to modern life, balancing their use is crucial for students' academic success and overall well-being. By setting boundaries, practicing digital detox, and using technology mindfully, students can mitigate the negative impacts while leveraging these tools for their educational and personal growth.

CHAPTER THIRTEEN

Unlocking the Value of Education: Inspiring the Resistant Student

This chapter delves into strategies and insights for parents and educators on how to engage with a student who is resistant to studying. It emphasizes the importance of approaching the conversation with empathy and understanding and provides a comprehensive set of points and examples tailored to resonate with disinterested students. The chapter also stresses the significance of inspiring rather than forcing, and how to help students see the intrinsic value of education in alignment with their interests and aspirations.

Convincing a student who is resistant to studying can be challenging, but it's important to approach the conversation with empathy and understanding. Here are some points that might help in explaining the importance of education, tailored to resonate with a student who is currently disinterested in studying:

1. Relevance to Everyday Life

- **Point**: Explain how education is not just about textbooks and exams, but about understanding the world. For instance, basic math helps manage finances, science explains how things work, and history teaches about the origins of our society.

- **Example**: Cooking requires understanding measurements (math) and chemical reactions (science), and planning a trip involves geography and budgeting skills.

2. Opens Up More Opportunities

- **Point**: Education broadens options for the future. Even if they're unsure about a specific career path now, having a solid educational foundation keeps more doors open.
- **Example**: Highlight stories of people who discovered their passion later in life, and how their education helped them pivot to these new paths.

3. Enhances Problem-Solving and Critical Thinking

- **Point**: Education develops critical thinking and problem-solving skills, which are valuable in any career and in everyday life.
- **Example**: Discuss how subjects like science and math teach us to analyze problems, think logically, and find solutions.

4. Provides a Safety Net

- **Point**: Even if the student has a non-academic career in mind, having an educational background can serve as a safety net.
- **Example**: An aspiring athlete or artist might face a highly competitive field; having a good education ensures there are alternative career paths available.

5. Helps in Understanding Current Events

- **Point**: Education helps in staying informed about the world and making sense of current events, which is crucial for being an engaged citizen.
- **Example**: Understanding political science helps in comprehending government decisions, and economics helps in understanding market trends.

6. Connects to Their Interests

- **Point**: Link their subjects to areas of personal interest or real-world applications they care about.
- **Example**: If they're interested in video games, explain the role of computer science and storytelling in game development.

7. Encourages Personal Growth and Development

- **Point**: Education is not just about academic growth, but personal development too – learning how to learn, how to research, and how to work with others.
- **Example**: Group projects and presentations can build teamwork and communication skills.

8. Necessary for Further Education and Training

- **Point**: Even if they wish to pursue vocational training or start their own business, basic education is often a prerequisite.
- **Example**: Culinary schools, coding bootcamps, or business courses all require foundational knowledge that comes from basic education.

9. Builds Confidence and Self-Esteem

- **Point**: Education can be empowering. Understanding various subjects and being knowledgeable can boost self-confidence.
- **Example**: The satisfaction of solving a complex math problem or writing a well-received essay can be significant confidence boosters.

10. Social Interaction and Networking

- **Point**: School and college are not just about studying; they are also about making friends, building networks, and learning social skills.
- **Example**: Many lifelong friendships and future business connections begin in educational settings.

Conclusion

- **Empathy and Understanding**: It's important to approach the conversation with empathy. Understand why they feel disinterested and address those specific concerns.

- **Inspiring, Not Forcing**: The goal is to inspire and motivate, not to force. Help them see the value of education in a way that resonates with their interests and aspirations.

CHAPTER FOURTEEN

A Journey of Sacrifice and Dedication

In the heart of every successful student's story lies an unsung hero—their parents. The sacrifices made and the unwavering dedication of parents often remain behind the scenes, hidden beneath the spotlight that shines on their children's achievements. In this chapter, we bring to you a poignant account of one such parent who stood by their child's side, navigating the tumultuous waters of education, ambition, and aspirations.

As you delve into this heartfelt narrative, you'll witness the sacrifices made, the challenges faced, and the unbreakable bond that exists between a parent and their child. This is a story of determination, resilience, and the unspoken love that propels a child toward success. It's a testament to the sacrifices parents make for the dreams of their offspring, and the dedication they exhibit in crafting a path to success, one step at a time.

Now, with utmost respect and authenticity, we present the journey in the exact words of the father. Each word you'll read is a reflection of his experiences, emotions, and unwavering support for his child within the chosen stream. This is a story that reminds us that behind every successful student, there stands a parent who sacrificed, supported, and believed in the power of dreams.

Join us as we embark on this touching journey, listening to the father's words that resonate with love, sacrifice, and dedication.

"I am who I am today because of the choices I made yesterday"

Eleanor Roosevelt, 1st Lady of United States of America (1933 to 1945)

In 2016, my son Soham Dasgupta was studying in Class 6 at New Era Senior Secondary School at Vadodara. We were staying together at our office colony at Vadodara with my younger son, Armaan Dasgupta and my wife, Mousumi Dasgupta. Away from our hometown Kolkata, we were getting used to the Gujarati cuisine and culture after my last stint at Rajasthan. I remember the difficulty in convincing my wife that we shall have a longer stay at Gujarat and thus Soham should take up Gujarati as 3rd language from Class 6 onwards. Who would have guessed the plans almighty had for us and Soham!!

In December 2016, our lives took an unexpected turn. Although, we estimated and expected a longer stay at Vadodara, God had already planned something else for us. Suddenly, I was offered a transfer to Bangladesh. I did not know what to expect from life. The role in Bangladesh was unexpected for me. Suddenly, we had to decide about movement of family, timing of movement, schooling, accommodation and so on. The anxiety was natural. I was not able to decide whether to shift family to Dhaka or keep them in India.

In January 2017, I moved to Dhaka while my kids and wife continued at office colony at Vadodara. My task was to find a good school for both kids, negotiate their transfer from Indian schooling system, work on best timing matching the curriculum, arrange a house for stay and decide on shifting of Soham, Armaan and Mousumi.

In April 2017, my family moved to Dhaka. Soham took admission in class 7 at a Dhaka school. Armaan took admission in Lower KG at a Dhaka school. After a stint of 4 years, in April 2021, my family returned to Kolkata. Soham completed his class 10 from Dhaka and was enrolled for class 11 at The Future Foundation School, Kolkata. He cleared 12th from the same school and currently pursing B.Tech (Electrical Engineering) at Indian Institute of Technology, Bombay.

Fast forward to December 2024, after 8 years, when I look back, I can recall the following challenges faced by our family at Bangladesh and our response towards them.

The Cambridge curriculum at Dhaka school was different than CBSE of India. The English was tough and so was other subjects. Soham struggled in the admission test for Class 7 due to the vast syllabus difference. I had to plead with the school management to grant us a three-month grace period. I promised that if Soham didn't meet their expectations within that time frame, the authority can issue a forced transfer. So, we decided to work on the studies for improvement for next few months.

Dhaka is a populous city with highly congested roads. On an average the travel time by car is around 5 KM per hour in Dhaka roads. The time taken to attend nearest tuition centre would have been 1.5- 2 hours each leg. So, Soham had to spent at least 5-6 hours if he had to attend a good coaching centre at Dhaka. This was in addition to normal school timing. My wife had to take care of my younger son at home, and it was not possible for her to drop him to a tuition centre. Thus, we had to drop the idea of availing any outside tuition for Soham.

My new assignment was demanding in Bangladesh. Moreover, I was in a private job and had multiple deliverables. Nevertheless, we had to make choice. We decided to motivate and support Soham for self-study without outside help. I had to find time for family. I had to give priority to family over work and I had to ensure continuation till class 10th at Dhaka (i.e. at least 4 years) without interruption in studies. We also decided to shift our both sons to Kolkata for 10+2 studies irrespective of my situation after 4 years of stay at Dhaka and work towards that. I discussed with my wife, and we decided to remain professionally content without chasing sky and devote time to sons.

To have an overlap with CBSE curriculum, I bought all the books from India for Soham and encouraged to follow the same. This was in addition to his school studies. We also tried to find his interest in the subjects. Although, we started with HCV's Physics and Cengage Maths, we were always apprehensive and was trying to discover his area of interest. I did some initial research and decided to start with Physics & Maths first from Class 8. I cannot forget those days - his everyday struggle in grasping the concepts and fighting spirit.

As time passed, I enquired Soham about his interests and aspirations with respect to engineering or medical. I remember that once he expressed his liking for biology, probably in class 10. I bought NCERT and solver books from India and discussed about the subject with him. However, we noticed that he struggled with biology, but he was a natural problem-solver. A series of discussion followed, and we concluded that he should pursue PCM (Physics, Chemistry, Mathematics) after Class 10. We left to him to pursue a career in Engineering or General Science. But we also urged him to learn more about IIT's in India and it's ability to transform an Individual. We wanted him to make a decision for an engineering career or medical career and helped him in his decision making process.

I remember, at some point in time in class 12, we faced challenges of multiple entrance exams like BITSAT, KVP and others. To alleviate his pressure, we decided to target only JEE Advanced and work towards that. We tried to keep the pressure away from him and avoided a burn out for him by appearing in multiple exams. We discussed with him and decided for putting 100% of JEEM'23 and JEEA'23 to make the best of it and not to dilute the efforts.

Beginning 2020 (Soham was in Class 9), I started doing CMA (Cost and Management Accountant) from ICMAI with an objective to co-study with him and develop my knowledge in commercial domain. I cleared Group 1 in Dec'20, Group 2 in Dec'21, Group 3 in Dec'22 and appeared for Group 4 in Dec'23. Continuous study helped me maintain focus and act as a parallel father cum co-student with Soham who he can follow and take inspiration in his painful IIT journey. Moreover, it removed my fear of studies and helped me to dig deep into his subjects and engage into a meaningful conversation with him. Also, it suited our long-term goal for helping him in his work or business after his graduation. My study and struggle were also aimed at helping him to realise that knowledge is a lifelong pursuit.

At home front, we maintained a simple lifestyle to minimize distractions and ensure that he valued every rupee earned. My wife played a pivotal role in teaching him the importance of money, effort and to live life with minimum resources. She also taught him not to spend without a reason. At home, we discussed and cultivated a constructive environment for growth, emphasizing the value of hard work and perseverance. Just to give an example, we managed to stay in a small flat at Kolkata with minimum resources and stayed grounded. Typically, the consumption guilt or need based buying is generally not common in kids born after 2000. So, we decided to instil the same in him thinking that in some way or other it will help him to manage cost of the company in his professional career.

I would like to state that it is the passion in you which will take you up and not money. I believe that when someone is brought up in abundant prosperity then probably nothing can make him or her happy, but it is the hardship which makes everlasting achievements.

I extend my thanks to all his teachers, family members and almighty God for helping him to achieve his passion. I seek blessings from everyone for us and pray that God's grace is showered on us.

CHAPTER FIFTEEN

"Voices of Success: Choosing Paths and Preparing for Triumph"

In this chapter, we bring you the voices of success—real-life stories from successful students who embarked on the journey of selecting their academic stream and walked the path of preparation with determination and purpose. These students come from diverse backgrounds, each pursuing different streams, but their experiences share a common thread: a passion for their chosen field, unwavering dedication, and a commitment to achieving their dreams.

Listen as they share their unique perspectives on how they navigated the decision-making process, overcame challenges, and found their way to success within their chosen streams. These voices offer invaluable insights and inspiration, showing that there is no one-size-fits-all approach to selecting a stream and excelling in it.

As you read their stories, you'll gain a deeper understanding of the thought processes, strategies, and sheer determination that have led these individuals to reach the pinnacles of achievement within their respective academic streams. Their journeys are a testament to the power of passion, perseverance, and the pursuit of one's dreams

Join us as we step into the shoes of these accomplished students, as they share their personal narratives in their own words. Their voices echo the message that with passion and dedication, you too can carve your own path to success within your chosen stream.

Srinjoy Ganguly (IIT Kharagpur)

My JEE journey commenced officially in 10th grade, but the groundwork began earlier. Accompanying my mother during her tuition sessions, I developed a keen interest in mathematics from a young age. I started solving school-level maths questions of classes 7 or 8 when I was studying in class 4 or 5. By 7th grade, I participated in the FIITJEE Big Bang Test out of curiosity, discovering JEE and the allure of engineering. Intrigued by the range of things to learn and of course the achievements of IITians, I joined FIITJEE to build my foundation. Throughout my preparation, I set small targets, including NTSE, KVPY, and Olympiads, for periodic self-assessment and motivation. In the process, I had to study a lot of things. Some topics were not as much interesting as others. Initially, I would not study those much, but later I realised that we need to cover those things to achieve a good score else that would drag us down. I went to ALLEN, Kota in class 11. It was the time of COVID. Mostly I had online classes, so self-discipline was very important. Regularly studying the class notes and revising the earlier ones are also very important. I sometimes felt that I should not take the regular tests as I lacked preparation. However, my teachers urged me to appear for the test irrespective of the level of preparation. I later understood that it makes us comfortable in the exam environment and helps us identify where our weaknesses are. Reviewing the question paper after the exam was one thing I felt helped me a lot. The biggest challenge in my preparation was COVID. I was infected 3 times and the last time it was just before JEE mains. I was hospitalized for several days. I had a minor stroke and for some moments I could not read anything. I was barely able to study or even wake up. I thought I would not be able to clear JEE advanced. My preparation was good and I was aiming for a good department in an old IIT, I thought it was all gone. However I decided to try and appear for JEE Advanced. I realised that I might have not been able to prepare at the end but my preparations earlier were quite good. I strategically attempted the paper and relied on my strong subjects. I made sure to clear the subject cutoff of every subject and maximize the score it in the easiest section. It was difficult but I cleared it. My experience is a lot different than others. I learned that every bit of our preparation is useful. We never know what happens at the end but if we study consistently with proper guidance then nothing can stop us from cracking the exam."

Suman (IIT Kanpur)

The reason why I chose Science after class 10 is because it was what I wanted to pursue in my future. I wanted to study Aerospace Engineering from a really young age and I had already started preparing for the IIT JEE Exams from class 9. I wanted to explore the thrills and challenges of an Engineering career and therefore I chose Science after class 10.

Shubham Raj
AIR- 579 (NEET 2020)

My journey of NEET exam

"Though my full-fledged preparation for NEET exam began in class 11 but its root goes to my school days. I had interest in maths and science since childhood. Also in RKM Vidyapith Deogarh(my school) there was competitive environment and there were many science enthusiasts, along with that sometimes some coaching institutes offered demo classes in between. So, science enthusiasts saw opportunities in form of NEET, AIIMS and JEE. In class 7 my biology was quite weak. So I started to study it properly. While being in class 9 and 10 I had explored biology of 11 and also of 12 to some extent; I had explored physics and chemistry of +2 to some extent too. So, in class 10 being equipped with these things I saw better opportunity towards medical side and also this job gives a lot of opportunities to serve people. These things motivated me to choose PCB in +2. I didn't choose maths because ultimately I would had to leave it at some point of time in my carrier and it would not be a wise choice to take maths just to clear board exams. For board exams I chose physical education since it is easy to cover it with understanding of biology.

In class 11, I moved to Allen Kota for full-fledged preparation(since Allen had good results and also there were good feedback from my friends who had explored some institutes). I was living in Kota with my mother, so basic problems of day to day life was not any issue for me and I could focus on my studies well. She had played an important role in my preparation by taking care of day to day problems.

For studies, I knew a very important thing that keeping 'backlogs' was the most important factor which would lead to stress and burden. So I always tried that before entering the next lecture of any teacher I should complete the homework and had understood the concept well. Also I did not miss classes. I had focused on- clearing my concepts, practising questions and having regular revisions. On weekends, I usually used to revise recent topics and regular tests helped me to revise previous topics too; if for some topic if I felt like that I had not touched them for a good amount of time then I just went through them.

I used combination of various methods of studies. Sometimes I revised through questions, sometimes just by recalling without any book, I also used to make charts and tables on paper for sticking it to wall so that I could see them even if I was not studying. They acted as stimulus for me to read a topic. I also used daily life things as stimulus to revise things like motion of wheel, fan, electric devices, construction sites, any plant etc.

In spite of these, there were certain topics which was problematic for me to remember and understand, like modern physics, capacitance, inorganic chemistry, GOC. To combat these I used following approaches: To clear concepts I contacted teachers and asked them the doubts which I was unable to understand after trying 2-3 times, and after that I used to solve questions. For clearing hurdle of inorganic chemistry and GOC, I had to go through contents and questions numerous times. NCERT also helped a lot especially in chemistry and biology.

Mnemonics also helped at many places to remember content. Topics in biology like Diversity, morphology, plant physiology also took numerous go through and solving questions.

In short, in my view this exam required clearing concepts, solving a lot of questions, many revisions, consistency and discipline to crack it nicely".

Aman Raj (IIT Patna)

"I'm quite good in mathematics from my childhood only... So it was already clear in my mind that I will choose mathematics in my class 12..after talking science i was focusing to do best in this field so i will choose iit as my destination after 12 so i started preparing for jee.. Actually I face some problem during my journey like sometimes i feel it quiet hectic but that's not in my hand so i just do my work consistently so things get better day by day... it's all about interest i really interested in maths so i don't focus on problems i just do my regular work under the guidance of my teachers...thanks "

Aarav Gupta (RMO Qualified), Class Xth

"Maths toh bachpan se favorite subject hua krta tha, toh phir naturally usmein zyada explore krne ka man Kiya tha, toh usse maths aur strong banti gayi, warna science ki baat kre toh phir woh bhi accha lgta tha, aur maths ke saath science Lena ek logical choice hoti hai, pr 9th 10th mein aake usmein bhi knowledge aur interest badhte rhe, Aur Olympiad ki prep krke Thora bahut pta chala ki "real maths" kya hoti hai, kyunki school maths kaafi narrow hota hai".

Rohit (IOQM qualified), Class XIth

Sir: Factors that got me into PCM were that first of all nobody forced but it was my choice ,and for those who are in 10th they should learn to enjoy the subject rather than just mugging up. and about Olympiad preparation I got to know about it from my neighbour bhaiya and fiitjee, and in Olympiad preparation and iitjee preparation there is a lot of difference first that Olympiad mainly focus on discrete mathematics and not calculative maths , so for preparation of Olympiad you have to focus on derivations of formula but not exact formula, and about hurdles in life there is only one sentence in my mind that carries me is discipline will get you there ,where motivation can't ,
Best of luck sir for your book".

Your Stream, Your Journey

As we reach the end of our journey through "Stream: Navigating Your Career Journey After Class 10," it's important to reflect on the invaluable insights, strategies, and guidance you've encountered in these pages. The path to selecting the right stream after Class 10 is a transformative journey, and it's one that you have the power to shape according to your unique passions, strengths, and aspirations.

Throughout this book, you've explored the importance of self-discovery, goal-setting, time management, effective study habits, and exam preparation within your chosen stream. You've learned about the different academic streams available in India – Science, Commerce, Arts, and Vocational – and how each offers its own set of subjects, career prospects, and pathways.

Remember that your choice of stream is not a binding contract; it's a starting point for your educational journey. Your interests and goals may evolve over time, and that's perfectly normal. Embrace change, be open to new opportunities, and stay committed to continuous learning.

Your stream is just one chapter in your lifelong learning adventure. As you embark on this path, keep in mind that your journey is uniquely yours. Each decision you make, each challenge you overcome, and each success you achieve contributes to the story of your life.

So, with an open heart and a curious mind, venture forth into the world of your chosen stream. Your potential is limitless, and your future is bright. Make the most of it, and remember that your dreams are within reach.

Let's unite and make a commitment to give our utmost effort to elevate our beloved nation, India, to a position of global leadership. Achieving this goal is possible only through the power of genuine education.

Jai Hind!

Author's Note

I want to express my heartfelt gratitude for accompanying me on this journey through the pages of "Stream." Writing this book has been a labor of love, fueled by the desire to empower students like you with the knowledge and confidence to make informed decisions about your future.

Choosing the right stream is a significant milestone in your life, and I hope that the guidance and insights shared here have been instrumental in helping you make that choice.

Always remember that you are capable of achieving greatness. Your talents and passions are unique, and the world is waiting for you to share your gifts with it. Pursue your dreams with dedication, resilience, and a hunger for knowledge.

I wish you all the best in your educational and career endeavors. May you find fulfillment, success, and happiness in the stream you choose and in every path you tread.

With warm regards,
SARVJEET KUMAR
Author of "Stream: Navigating Your Career Journey "

Additional Resources

To further assist you on your journey, here are some additional resources that you may find helpful:

Career Guidance Counselors: Reach out to career guidance counselors at your school or educational institutions for personalized advice.

Online Career Assessment Tools: Explore online tools and assessments to gain insights into your interests, aptitudes, and potential career paths.

Educational Websites: Visit reputable educational websites for information on various academic streams, colleges, and entrance exams.

Books: Continue to expand your knowledge by reading books related to your chosen stream or area of interest.

Online Courses: Consider enrolling in online courses to enhance your skills and knowledge in specific subjects or fields.

Peer and Alumni Networks: Connect with peers and alumni who have pursued similar academic streams or careers for guidance and mentorship.

Professional Organizations: Join relevant professional organizations or clubs related to your stream to network and stay updated on industry trends.

Career Fairs and Workshops: Attend career fairs and workshops to explore different career options and interact with professionals in your field.

Remember that your educational journey is a continuous process of growth and self-discovery. Use these resources to support your aspirations and make informed decisions as you progress in your chosen stream.

"Just give your best and wait for the rest ....."

www.ingramcontent.com/pod-product-compliance
Lightning Source LLC
LaVergne TN
LVHW041123150826
845673LV00007B/2165